SOFT PAGES

A poetry Compilation

PHUMLA XUZA KHANYILE

CLASSIC AGE PUBLISHING
Published by Classic Age Publishing
271 Kent Avenue,
Randburg,
2193
South Africa

www.classicagepublishing.co.za

First Published by Classic Age Publishing (South Africa) (Pty) 2016

ISBN: 978-0-9947069-1-1

Cover design by Galluh
Proofread and Typesetting by Vukulu Sizwe Maphindani

DEDICATION!

The *Soft Pages* you hold in your hands is a compilation of heartfelt poems inspired by the heart's desire to be heard. The title was inspired by Poem 45 on the book and also by certain profound words I came across by chance in a letter written by Harper Lee to Oprah Winfrey in May 2006 - those words emphasized the relevancy and ongoing need to jot words down on soft pages rather than on metal (technology gadgets).

…And, Oprah, can you imagine curling up in bed to read a computer? Weeping for Anna Karenina and being terrified by Hannibal Lecter, entering the heart of darkness with *Mistah Kurtz*, having Holden Caulfield ring you up — some things should happen on soft pages, not cold metal.

Source: http://www.lettersofnote.com/2012/10/some-things-should-happen-on-soft-pages.html *Soft Pages'* my message to every woman, young and old who has gone or yet to go through similar life challenges. Through these inked pages the message is simple "you are more than your circumstances; you have it in you to rise above your storms…"

A special dedication to my mother, *Nowinile Caroline Xuza* – my pillar of strength and anchor. I am solid and sound because of your guidance and forever unwavering support. May the good God shield you and strengthen your, to live long and see the fruits of your work in me. *Enkosi Ndalakazi!*

To my children *Sibusiso, Cebolenkosi* and *Wandile*! I am the woman and mother I am today because I have you. I thank God for placing you in my love and care and through our experiences; I am learning every day to be a better person. Truly you have raised me!

I am also thankful to every soul that crossed my path! I am who I am today because of all the experiences through various encounters. You have all contributed in my journey, whether be in joyfulness or tears, good or bad times.

A special thank you to the angels in human form who grew faith in my pen leaps and bounds by buying my first book, Love Notes, all I can say is "see the work of thy deeds."

As an African adage goes *"umntu ngumntu ngabantu"*
– Indeed, No man is an island!
Thank you for letting me bud and blossom in your midst.

Contents

20. Guy somewhere

21. God teared

22. Heal me time

23. Hopeless man

24. Humble eagle

25. I am here

26. I need a friend

27. In your palm

28. It rained

29. It will pass

30. Kind words

31. Letting go

32. Look of love

33. Lost love

34. Mamelodi

35. Miles and tons

36. My First time

37. Of age

38. One of the kind

39. Pace

40. Passing shadow

A BETTER STAND

We're the charter of promises

A prophesy long written

We're a shadow of things hoped for

A reality we all fought for

We are the planted seeds

Watered by tears, by blood

With sticks, with stones thrown

With chanted painful songs

We are a generation of hope

Heirs of sacrifices

Of defiance turned to compliance

We are healers of the past ills

So let's raise our fists

To the sons and daughters

Warriors with no shields

Those who took a stand

We salute their unselfish efforts

Their backs bended to bridges

Ushers of a better tomorrow

Heroes who died with a dream

Here and now we pledge

Never to come short of their hopes

Never to take for granted the cost

Always to remember the price paid

We stand united on a bridge of promises

Rewriting each tainted page with a better ink

Reconciling our differences at peace

With no stones thrown, no bullets shot

A CHILD

These eyes have seen things

Shades of beauty and sadness

These eyes have watered tons

Yet I am still a child

Beyond my years plenty I've seen

Things ought to have been hidden

In the window of my soul they glare

In the pages of my memories, written

Dare not look away from my plight

Although scared am still a child

Beyond these fragile walls

Lies a child in need of love and care

Throw me no crumbs and pained looks

These only last till your smile wanes

Turn not your back and walk away

Take my hand lead the way home

I am a child in the midst of chaos

With turmoil housed in my pleading eyes

Dare not tarnish further my innocence?

I only come to you in need

I am a child in need of love

Look beyond the visible scars

My soul limps for your care

For loving hands to sew me whole

A FRIEND

I may not be there to hold your hand

To stand beside you to share your joys

I may not wipe your tears when you're sad

To flank you along with your peers

But you must know I'm still your friend

I am your friend though at a distant

I know not your scars but I feel your pain

Your words speak deep to my heart

I need not see you to call you a friend

In my heart I feel and that's enough

I am your friend this I know

If not I wouldn't care to know your name

Nor see your face in the midst of crowds

I call you my friend despite the age

And this I need not add to any page

I heard the echoes of your streams

Running waters that never dry

You called me through the blowing winds

With the name my forefathers gave

I sniffed your sweat beneath my perfumed flesh

A familiar fragrance that refused to let go

It reminded me of your majestic hills

Suddenly healing all my known ills

Nostalgia rose its horn like a yeasted dough

Concrete walls posed as your jungles

Paved streets turned to dusty footpaths

I smelled your burning fires from running engines

Africa you have beckoned me home

Out of the city I come at a hurried pace

To the valleys I've long stridden

To splash in your cool virgin streams

It is you who knows my true nakedness

By my bare footedness you're not amazed

Have I not paced in your fertile soils?

Tripping and landing on your gravels

How I miss to be awakened by the crow of the cock

If not by falling droplets from a sweaty roof

To walk leisurely in the dewy grass

To be greeted by not so friendly barks

Africa upon you I laid my trust

Never to be detached from your cord

Am I not the seed of your loins?

Unto your bowels I will come to lie

A HEROES' CLIMB

When heroes gather

Post battles won

Of successes achieved

In glitter and splendour

They count not their losses

Yet it is a norm

Cowards lick their wounds

Their scars they count

Unto heaps that pains

Just as to their failures cling

When climbers climb

Up the rugged inclines

With cliffs that fatally hangs

Upon deadly curves and bends

It is but to the top they aim

The good we seek

Comes not at ease

Nor it dwells within our reach

The steeper the climb

The nearer the great end

When heroes gathers

Those who worked so hard

Defying all known odds

Nor succumbing to their fears

They shall chant their victory song

A LETTER TO MY EX

This letter I pen from the heart

It is of words I long kept

Suppressed beneath all pretence

As I daily live as if with no cares

It would not kill me to admit

So many times you cause me to flinch

Seeing that you happily gone

While in my memory you painfully dwell

How many times must I turn away?

Each time in her arms you cross my path

I could still hear your happy laughs

Causing a soft tap to fall off my eyes

How can you be so cruel?

Flaunt and gloat at my expense

To erase me just like an error

As if our hands never twined

Of all the paths you choose to take

Why should it be mine you cross?

Is it to ignite my pain?

Or to spite me with shame?

Of you this I ask

Remember I still have a heart

Though you have elected to part

I can still feel the hurt

It is well you found new love

But why must I cheer on your behalf

Who will nurse my pain and loss?

Wait a bit for my turn to dance

If I were to talk for the dead

The lying souls that talk no more

Those we loved and held so dear

My sister would top the list

'I have gone too soon she would say'

At her prime she lost her life

The bullets flew and pierced her skull

Tears flew from eye to eye

My mother wailed with a broken heart

The beauty of our home was plucked

I could almost hear her cheerful laugh

As she waltzed from room to room

'Mother care for a cup of tea' she would ask

From here to there sweeping the mess

Just as she did before she died

If my late sister would yet talk again

'I could have been a mom', she would say

'I could have been a nurse or a singer

I missed seeing my siblings grow

Or be there for my aging mom'

'I could have wailed at my father's grave

Cried tears of joy at birth of your children

But am not there, am gone

My picture is no longer on the wall

But keep me in your hearts still'

'Here beyond I am at peace

My killer is now my neighbour

Over feasts we mended our cracks

Forgive him too, he paid the price'

She would say as she waves and fades

BEATEN

Swollen eyes

They did not see eye to eye

Bruises all over her arms
She could not hid the harm

Her screams echoed

To many ears heard

She wailed in fear

While begging in tears

She's been beaten

Beyond recognition

So lame is the reason

No logic in the excuses

Did he not claim to love?

By his hands he harmed

He spilled her blood

As if she was not worth a dime

Beaten by her love

Ridiculed in the neighbours' eyes

How will she walk with pride?

They all heard her cries

Beaten with aggression

As if by hateful hands

How could this be?

The one vowed to forever love

She is so scarred

In and out

Her faith shattered

She no longer trust love

She sees in half

From her swollen eyes

She keeps so mum

He broke her jaws

Jail bird caught and caged

So silent is your song

No more room for you to fly

Beautiful flower in a small pot

Confined in a little corner spot

Dare not let your beauty fade

Shifting shade of the oak tree

Under your branches many dwell

Yet alone so tall you stand

Waters from crystal streams

Forever running without a pause

When will you take your rest?

Take a halt and see therein

Beauty you seek is not too far

All is implanted in your petals

Break the confines that cage your mind

Sing and fly up above the skies

It is no sin to love self a little more

BROKEN STONES

They claim to know you well
Yet stones they throw your way
Some claim to fix your flaws
Yet only God knows your fears

To some you just a broken stone
Not worth to be picked and joined
To some an obstacle on their path
Yet to God you're precious to add

Though broken many times
To fragments that rapidly peels
It is a mending hand you need
More than the judging crowds

God knows your silent cries

He long read your hidden mind

Have you not heard him call?

Guiding your steps along the way

God is great this I know

He who values broken stones

How many times has he picked you up?

Trusted in you despite your flaws

Oh mending broken stones

In God's hands you're safely kept

He heals your past and path your future

He is the hope worth the trust

BUTTERFLIES

Butterflies flying up above the skies

In every wall climbing to plant kisses

On window seals taking peeks

So beautiful they are in their coloured coats

Butterflies on stretched-out fields

Lonely they seem to journey

From stem to stem

As if to spread across a word

Butterflies oh beautiful creatures

Small and intriguing in your make

How did you creep into my belly?

I feel your little wings flap as he comes

It is all beautiful and colourful in my heart

So full and deep is the feeling within

Butterflies dance and flap to the tune of love

Every time he whispers my name

CELIBACY

What is celibacy?

If not a lonely cage unlocked

A book with torn pages

A heart tried and tested

Is it not a fight of defiance with self?

To shun desires once felt

A look away from fun felt

A new chapter to pen

Some say it is a lonely windy road

With curves that twist and turns

And slopes that face the edge

Only the strong mount to the end

Unto me it is rather moments with self

A self-made space for solitude with self

To preserve one from hurt and shame

To page a clean page to write upon

There is a place where all herd

Lit bright by golden lights of hope

A home of dreamers in pursuit

A hub in *Africa* where most flock

From dusty to paved streets they rush

A vibrant heart beating life to the south

Welcome to *Jo'burg* the city of lights

They come bearing hopes and dreams

With not much at hand but zeal

Driven by desire to succeed

Yet many are swallowed by its walls

Oh city that flourishes from pain

In you it is a man for himself

Those who slacks sleep on streets

Like a *Jezebel* you attract to imprison

The young and old get lost in your sub-ways

With tunnels and bridges made homes

As dagga smoke coils up to a dark cloud

Some win yet many turn to the unknown

Bodies lying cold in nameless graves

Of tales left untold and chapters unclosed

Jozi so you are affectionately called

A city of gold with rusty streets

Of history written in walls and street poles

Bearing names of those who once lived

On lanes that leads to the places near and far

Carrying souls from worlds apart

A home to girls who lost all hopes

Warn your sons and daughters

Lest the glitter swallow their youth

Jo'burg streets are not made of gold

So icy are they in winter nights

Ask those they housed and froze

With so majestic sky-scraping walls

So lowered are standards in your streets

COMMA

Stuck in a comma

Death only a full stop away

Voices echoing near and far

Divine forms hovering about

Hosanna song chanted louder than a sigh

My brother sat in sadness

Tears flooding and clouding

Holding on to my lifeless hands

Whispering forbidding words

Begging I should not dare end

Mother on her frail knees

Weeping and pleading to the Lord

Offering herself instead

Yet slowly I sank to a deep blue hole

All the things loved fading in a distant

Up the hill with crowds we climbed

Up in a float beyond a bed of clouds

The Song of Songs louder with every hike

Past the crystal streams to the pearl paved way

Unto a home of homes with golden gates

Emmanuel stood holly with open arms

To usher us through our eternal home

In his hand a book of life he held

Page by page he called the names

Yet my name was never found

A voice roared like a thousand seas

Dear daughter it is not yet your time

Go back to make amends

You've been spared to live more

The gates were closed the curtains fell

The deep blue hole spew me whole

Back to the world of tears and pain

My brother still held my hands so tight

My mother wet my face with tears cold

They were so glad I was awake at last

FAREWELL HURT

I will not shed another tear

Lest to flood my soul

Enough sorrows! No more!

Find another slave to hold

I refuse the sting of pain

This heart has long endured

Almost to a state of being numbed by sobs

Farewell hurt I take a hike

Goodbye, it is time we part

May our paths never cross

Walk, never look back

I know you'll not be missed

FLAKES OF LOVE

When love breaks

Into flakes and pieces

That pierce the heart

That bleeds the soul

Joy waves into distant places

It takes yet another love

To heal and mould

To find and keep

A love that builds

A love heals wounds

When love melts to rivers of regrets

Gathering to pour to lakes of sorrows

It takes yet another surge of love

To path a way to streams of joy

Restoring hope once known

When love breaks

Into fragments, into portions

Collapsing the heart into muddy puddles

Hope crumbles and fades

Only for a leap of faith to rise you from ashes

FLICKER OF HOPE

Flicker of hope

Why burned just for a while

So many things I should have said

Just like that your spark died!

Hope that graced my horizons

Why take beauty from my eyes

The view was worth the watch

Now gloom dwells in my fore

Eagle that flew me in my dreams

To places of splendour far

Unforgettable adventures of the heart

You've left a deep hollow in my gut

Farewell light that dwelled at end of my tunnel

Beautiful star that shot and shined

Fly up to explore the skies

In my heart you'll forever have a home

FORGIVEN

For so long I hold a drudge

So heavy it weighed me down

The heart carved a million times

With an evil eye I held you afar

I held my self a slave to things that passed

Of words and thoughts that broke me down

Of walls of anger that kept me in

Did I not end up hurting most?

I have reached a point of letting go

Tired I am of sleeplessness nights

Of gloomy days with tearful eyes

I am letting go of hurtful thoughts

No more tears to cloud my eyes

Nor achy heart to slow me down

Here now I cleanse my heart

I forgive you, I set me free

GRAVITY

Why keep dragging me down

Despite desire to fly up above

Why remind me of the ground

When the skies are open wide

Gravity you can't pin me down

Not against my will dare not try

Am going up no matter what

My name will be written amongst the stars

What is all this noise about?

Is it wrong to dream so big?

To seek to climb up to the high

Don't I always come down?

GUY SOMEWHERE

Beyond mountains on the West

Along the stretching coastal sands

On rock beds that for centuries spread

A guy on hat lies on their solid backs

He stands magnificent and tall

Parading his masculine self to the sea

If only the waves could utter words!

To the sea mini creatures he's a demi god

On a stone throne overlooking their world

The waves ushers the winds to pay homage

They swiftly blow and bow to a whirr

His long feet pace the shoreline

Leaving a trail of prints on wet sands

Thought they last for but a while

Creeping waters wash them back to the sea

In his eyes distance he has covered

Past the roaring waves of the dividing sea,

Across stacks of rugged mountains in his fore

To a place where his heart longs

A home on the East where he belongs

The wind gently hug his longing heart

As the sea gulls sings a calming song

As if to reassure he bruising heart

Somewhere along the sea he finds his peace

GOD SHED TEARS

God's tears are falling

From the skies they're pouring

Heaven gates are wide opened

His sorrows soak the world

What have we done?

To grieve a heart so big

Heavenly tears are pouring

Upon men and women

Upon good and bad

He cries out with a roar

The world is such amazed

The young and old are dazed

Unto silence they all coil

Who will comfort the comforter?

God is shedding tears

HEAL ME TIME

Nothing stays the same

Time ushers change

Even sorrows wave

Unto the heart all things are buried

Into deep and shallow graves

Yet as time passes the sting fades

Nothing stays the same indeed

Gloom shifts for happiness

Clouds of doom will surely clear

A new day comes with joyful noise

Tears will dry from the eyes

Sadness will depart from your heart

Nothing that is will forever remain

Peace will make in you a perfect stay

Pain felt will slowly melt way

HOPELESS MAN

Man with no hope

He who walks without faith

Down a road that knows not his fate

Hidden behind a mask of failure

Tarrying behind the judging crowds

Swallowed by his own regrets

In his world the sun no longer sets

Gone is the sweet breeze ushering hope

Fear is now his constant friend

He drags his feet and shattered self

Up and down the streets without resolve

With his head always down

Man who dares not dream again

He who lives to battle with his doubts

Unto self-defeat he now succumbs

HUMBLY EAGLE

What can I say?

"Death be shamed"

You steal from our eyes but not in our hearts

You've taken a good soul but you have not won

Death that snatches our own

He was an epitome of humbleness

A man of substance who threw not his weight

Oozing respect towards young and old

Amongst names, his has been called

To grace heavens with his presence

Cry not dear friends he ran his race

Unto the Lord he now rests

Fly oh great humbly eagle

Fly to your eternal home

Heavenly hosts awaits to usher you in

The Lord has made feast to honour you

I AM HERE

Confine me not to time and spaces

I am silent though filled with words

I choose to walk alone in crowds

Singing a solo in a choir's song

If you see me not, am not gone

I am hidden in open plains

I need not be loud to be heard

Listen to the sound of passing winds

I am standing despite countless falls

Define me not by crowds that flocks

My voice is loud above the chaos

From a distance I opt to watch

Seek me not in painted pictures

Nor in words jotted in past times

I cannot be found in strangers' faces

Or locked in cabinets of memories

I NEED A FRIEND

All I need is a friend

Someone to share my world

To dwell in my sacred plains

Him I can lean and trust

For he is not quick to judge

Nor always ready to up and quit

All I need is a friend

This world is too unkind

How can I walk a lonely lane?

Too long is the journey faced

With all the so loud silent thoughts

Chaotic are strangers' voices

All I need is a friend

Broadest shoulders to lean on

Someone to hear out my fears

Not make mockery of my flaws

A reliable emphatic soul

Him who can lay low the human guard

IN YOUR PALM

Does destiny lie?
In the paths on your palm
Is there truth in those curved lines?
Or are they just fabricated lies

If you give me your hand
Will it show where it all leads
Can these lines really tell why?
Or where it shall all end

Can I read on your palm?
What our tomorrow brings
Is it mapped out in your hand?
Or is it the mind that lies

If life was all written in our hands
Traced in every cutting line
Why would it take the mind?
Just to read what lies in the palm

Let me read on your palm

Maybe it can save us time

Spare me from harm that comes

If not keep all my fears calmed

It Rained

Oooh it rained beyond soft showers

Sorrows poured into muddy puddles

It flooded into torrent of emotions

The heart roared thunders that cracked

Lighting tore the face into segments

Leaving ruins from eroded feelings

She sniffed and gasped to catch her breath

Her heart she clutched in a crouch

Deep she sank in a wail that wet her chest

Though the rain came to a halt at last

It brought not a rainbow belt

She lay face-flat in her lake of sorrows

Her eyes are dry but not her heart

For years to come she'll still share the tears

She'll still wail for the scars left

It will pass

When life turns a tide

And toss you up and down

Hold on to the promise of time

It will surely usher you calm

When life spins you like a coin

To a point you can't tell your head from tail

Though gravity fights to pull you down

Hold on to the anchoring hope

Oh Yes all will come to pass at last

Even in the midst of storms

That often fall without a halt

There is always a brief pause

Hold on it will pass

This pain that seems too great

Each passing day the sore gathers

In time only a scar will remind

KIND WORDS

Say kind words

Even if only one word

Surely you'll not lose a dime

Nor will you part with your pride

In the world that is so broken

Say words to heal the fallen

Send kind words to the forsaken

Preach words to heal the weakened

Tell words of kindness to the world

The ear desires to hear counsel

Tire not to lend a saving hand

To multitudes who needs to be heard

Say a word, a kind word

Words that saves a broken soul

Though not tagged with a price tag

They are worth the world to the one who hears

LETTING GO

I will not hold it against you

Though sad and sore

The heart has its own will

Often it rebels against own wishes

I've sat in that seat of decision before

My own pits and falls I've seen

So many hearts I've cracked and peeled

Just to please my heart's will

I guess I should let you go

You no longer feel the same

What is the use to tail you with pleas?

You've said your peace now farewell!

I will not hold it against you

I set you free with no hope you'll return

Your heart deserves to have its wish

Even if mine bears the pain of loss

LOOK OF LOVE

Flawless eyes of love

Beauty they see in plain

Faith they hold where none dwells

Naked and pure is your view

Some claim these eyes are blinded

For they trust and believe

Persuade and pursue

Eyes that see beyond flaws

Look at me with eyes of love

Past the posture and the form

Beyond confines of hips and curves

Look at me with flawless eyes

I stand before love unmasked

Tear down walls of my defence

See me beyond all pretence

Defeat me with the look of love

LOST LOVE

Tears drop to a fountain fall

Down they fall to lakes and ponds

The heart collapse to pain so great

It is so hard to say goodbye

It is love gone cold

No longer holds on to its own

It fails to rise post the storms

Tears fall to floods of loss

Sadly the end has now come

To break the pact, to part the ways

Sorrows descend in heavy hail

Tears run to formless streams

The time has come to wave

To worlds apart, to distant past

Oh such despair, the love lost the spark

Tears drop, pillows wet

Mamelodi, Mother of Melody!

What melodies lace your lips?

Oh home to thousands of voices

Do you whistle like a bird?

Calling upon the scattered to gather?

Or it is just to your amusement you hum

So melodic is your name

Though am so unfamiliar to your streets

You sure sound like a home worth a pace

Where one can quench a thirst

Without Paul Kruger statue on the face

Mamelodi, home that house a lot

How many legends have you spewed?

I smell ecstasy in your skies

Emitting from countless joyful sounds

Towards heavens coiling up like a cloud

Yet history tells of your fair share of pain

Like many you lost sons and daughters

Your streets got tainted by their blood

Nevertheless you rose from the ashes

Your heroes never fought in vain

Like a blanket of many colours

So beautiful is your diversity

Nationalities come and dwell

To many you are a true home

Like a mother you embrace them all

What melodies spring from your chords?

Oh bird that flies up above the skies

What is the source of your jubilation?

You seem to float above your tribulations

Defiant to the past that holds back

Mamelodi, the mother of all melodies sang!

MILES AND TONS

In case the winds of time

Chase memories with tides

I'll catch your glimpse in my mind

In the chamber of thoughts that won't die

Not even a thousand miles

Could wipe away your smile

Though I may cry a tons of tears

I can never run dry of your love

Now I walk in the lane so alone

My heart a chest to your corpse

Gone is the joyful whispering winds

The love melody no longer lives in me

Winter days have long descended

The sun no longer shines the brightest

I lie awake pained in shadows

My thoughts the only voice loudest

Sorrows have in me a home found

I long for summer days to come

Sun rays to creep into my heart

Melting away the cold stones of doubt

Sweeping away all my fallen leaves

I know I'll bud like a rooted stump

Time will dry the ooze of my wounds

My face will glow like the moon

To the ocean emptiness will go

MY FIRST

Making love the first time

Like icy rain from the sunny skies

With the sun still blazing

While clouds kept melting

I shivered

All the tales often told

Sweetness of passion Bespoken

The love, the tenderness

Got torn into tiny pieces

I teared

Anticipation plus confusion

Fear laced by excitement

Sweet torture

Prolonged climax

I pained

My first time was my last

To all the bestowed innocence

Invasion of my womanhood

Harvesting of my vineyard

Possession of my mind

ONE OF THE KIND

I have seen them come and go

They swore to be best of friends

Wait until a cloud descend

They dare not bid farewell

When we met faith I had lost

A friend was but a hollow word

There was no one for me to trust

But you are one of the kind!

Dear friend you awesome

Friends like you are hard to find

I am honoured to call you my own

In you I have learned to believe

Ours is an affair that covers miles

Years have passed, still we smile

Just two hearts that chose to fit

Of all the friends, you're the best

Thank you pal for being my friend!

Of age

Gone are the days of lullabies

Accept I am a woman now

In my prime, ready to go

To compose a song of my own

Daddy's little has now grown

She has now found joy

Beyond confines of her father's heart

Outside the gates of his compound

She has found a man who shares her dreams

A son in-law to bring home

To keep her safe when storms rise

But you are still her knight

She'll miss you most when shadows falls

Your tales of old told on the home porch

Of strangers turned to friends of all

Timeless, you'll always be

PACE

The journey is mine to walk

No matter how long it takes

Judge not my pace

All in good time it'll pay

In this journey my life I page

Learning of all things that pains

Finding new ways to paint

Rubbing away the past

This journey is mine to take

Alone in my pace

Lest the crowds slow my pace

I still want to hear my heart pace

I know your high hopes

Dreams attached alike

But tis my path to choose

Lest I blame you for my faults

PASSING SHADOW

You came in a sudden rush

Oh passing shadow that dashed

You walked pass like driven winds

Just as a dissolving dream does

Into fragments of events

A puzzle of disjoined thoughts

I thought I held you in my palm

Safe and secured in my heart

Yet like a bird you long flew

Leaving a lonely cage behind

With broken shells of a sad heart

With questions piled unanswered

You were a passing shadow

Out of nowhere you came

Back to the wall you faded

Within a twinkle of an eye

Leaving a thousand cries

With hands stretched out wide

You were not here to stay

You never intended to remain

Back to the end of the world you rushed

I cannot even trail your scent

Only for a little while I held your hand

But your heart I never had

PRAYER FOR THE POETS

I pray for the minds

Often pregnant with words

For the messenger's mouth

Often itched to proclaim

I pray for the poets

He who knows not the source

Yet in him runs a stream of wisdom

Some say she's too deep

Some dismiss her as wordy

Yet he has a gift of the word

Bless the beautiful poets

Though they move with grace and majesty

They spit raw truth

Buying no faces to spare the facts

No matter the cost truth they speak

May your minds be forever green?

In all seasons see your showers fall

The fountain of wisdom in you forever run

May it spill over in your own lives!

Be fertile and rich with your own words

Raped

Is it the penetration that defines?

The tattered clothes lying about

She aches from all around

From wounds dug in and out

Is it how rudely the perpetrator took?

Despite the pleas abruptly silenced

What cause it a heinous crime?

Is it how she was laid down in the mud?

Is it because it was a stranger

What about the friend who did the same

A trusted father, an uncle or a brother

Did it make a difference who harmed?

The thought assaults my mind

It causes my tummy to twist to knots

The pain of it all slices the mind

How much more it dices the one defiled

She has been raped and shamed

Pass the tearing of her tattered cloth

Beyond bruises on her achy thighs

She has been stripped naked of her pride

In the pool of her own tears and blood

Her pride became a mat of shame

She lied naked against her will

While someone unkind took her joy

REALITY SLAP

With such a slap across the face

You woke me up from a daze

Pricking my beautiful bubble

A house of my fictions

I knew you were a glass house

Bound to crush from a mere throw

Yet I nursed this fragile cup of thoughts

Despite how naïve they felt

Reality check you fell hard on my lap

Out of the blue, just like that

Was it a sin to smile a bit?

Must you always crack me with your whip?

Reality though I kept you at bay

You couldn't wait to come my way

Without civility nor a thought

You threw yourself at my fore

RESTORATION

On stone cold floors we kneel

Hear our needs as we pray

Pardon our weekly flaws

Weed out the seeds of sin

Mend our souls we plead

The Lord that heals us

In all forms of sicknesses, restore

In broken homes, descend

Pillar the falling, strengthen the weak

Guide us back home we pray!

Let the ailing ear in death bed, hear

The drunk hearts in all corners, sober up

Speak self-love to the harlot on the street

Talk change to the criminal in jail

Rebuke poverty rebuild our wealth

Like a seed falling on a fertile soil

Nourish our souls with sweet words

Plant your will in our minds

Write your truth in our hearts

Ceaselessly we'll sing you praises

RUMOUR HAS IT

I heard it from the grapevine

Rumour has it you've found the one

They've seen her in your arms

Your love for her is one of its kind

She begins and ends your smile

She truly shines your eyes

They say you head over heels in love

You even trail her steps in the dark

Rumour has it you've blinded your eyes

Tis her only you opt to see

She is the cause of your joy

She is the bright of your day

I heard it from the grapevine

You knelt on your knee to plea

It was in the mid of the day

You did not care who mind

It must be love fuelling your zeal

They've seen you paled by her tears

Just as you've blossomed at her smile

She truly owns your heart

Rumour has it you're at your happiest

To you, life has been so kind

Gone are your days of sorrows

I have been buried in your yester years

It only befits to wish you well

Time has come to say goodbye

I hope she loves you so always

That you'll never have to regret

SCARS

Deep scars hidden to the eye

Though not carved by no sharpened blade

But by words and by deeds

To no end causing to bleed

Scars beyond the surface plains

Invisible to the human eye

Yet so known to the heart

For their pain is too great

Scars carved in the heart

With time you'll slowly fade

By kind words and deeds you'll heal

Though your marks will forever stay

SCENT OF DEATH

Morning glory you've departed

Dear night you've lost your shine

Wind why blow without a whistle

Why is death a new scent of roses?

Before me lies broken pieces

Of dreams and hopes shattered

The heart consumed by pain

Sorrow is now my new blanket

Oh time why did you not alert

Horizon you held back the signs

I would have cherished more

Loved and held her high

Death a great offence you've done

I am now a man without a will

A dead rose on a broken stem

My heart you've split in half

SLEEK TONGUE

Sugar-coated are your lies

Though I get pangs of suspicion

So nicely you pack them

In colourful alluring heaps

So swift is your deceit

With empty coloured words

With silly yet charming deeds

Yet deep I fall despite the doubt

You carved them into melting flakes

Of shadows of reality that do not last

Your crafty mouth coats them nice

Into vanishing hopes and dreams

So dangerous is your sleek tongue

It speaks enticing lies that entangles

So often you tied me hands and knees

Yet I still line up for more of your lies

SOFT PAGES

Here is to you an open book to read

Take a peek at every page

Tell me what do you see?

Can you comprehend?

Though hardened are the covers

So soft are the pages

Read me line by line

The lines in-between are all blank

What you see is what you get

Indulge me on your feelings

Where you not sure, let me know

Forget about what others say

I am the dusty book on the bottom shelf

Passed by many without a glance

Though rugged still beautiful are my pages.

SOMEDAY

So tired I am of 'someday'

It is good as 'down the line'

Someday is a promise without hope

I can no longer hold on to a promise

To rely on a day yet to come

What if someday never comes?

Someday rings louder to my mind

This word I heard countless times

While time slowly passes me by

How many someday' must come to pass?

Just to bring me close to the day

Why the use such a delaying world

THAT 'Y' DAY

I long for the day

When tea is so milky

Sheets are so silky

And you're so cuddly

My mind runs to the day

When all things go smoothly

Thoughts flood sweetly

And you smile cutely

But truth is so sneaky

You are so picky

My heart feels achy

Yet you still make me happy

Am I so silly?

To think you are so sexy

Though you've been so nasty

Treating me so coldly

The day will come

When you'll be so mushy

Give me your love fully

And I'll be yours wholly

THE BEGGAR

He is more than a beggar

That stands on a street corner

Although he asks for little coins

His life tells a lot more

From his rugged clothes

With holes and patches

The long un-kept beard

With the head uncombed

He who defied the norm

To dwell in his own home

He rather live in the wild

Anywhere his head he can lay

Is he not someone's son?

A brother or even a father

What chased him from his home?

What made him face the cold?

He is more than a beggar

His life is a story untold

Of dreams deferred

Of hopes shattered

So gloom is the picture

Yet he is the most resilient

He faithfully stands on one spot

Waiting to receive from judging eyes

What has killed his will?

What broke his spirit so?

Who chased him from home?

Questions he never answers

Is he is not a reminder to those who look

To count their blessings as they pass

To hold on to hope no matter the storms

To value the little comfort no matter the costs

He is more than just a beggar

He is a man on a mission

A lesson to be learned

A reason to hold on.

THE LEARNER

Who said growth knows confines

Have I not grown each passing day?

Beyond the limit of my bones

Past the teachings of my folks

Have I not new lessons learned?

I dare not claim to know it all

Though many curves I've turned

Has life not proven me otherwise?

Stumbled face flat by my own pride

I still have a lot to learn

It seems pain from betrayal knows no age

Disappointments you cannot outgrow

The heart will take its lesson till the end

As wisdom faces its tests to the end

And I will forever be a learner

Bear with me and my mistakes

Forgive me for my weaknesses

I am not the best you wished

What if tomorrow brings change?

All you need to do is wait

I do not claim to be beyond reproach

In learning mistakes are often made

But bear with my errors and flaws

Time will erase them all

One by one I'll replace them all.

THE NIGHT

When the night slowly pass

Yet the sleep fails to come

Countless thoughts descend

Of things silently wished

Of desires yet to unfold

When the sleep escapes at night

And the mind takes a voyage

To faces lost in a distant past

Of friends missed and lovers lost

The night turns to battle of thoughts

I slowly drift to the plains beyond

On a fertile field of long held desires

Of fantasies sowed as bed of roses

In colourful painted pictures on the walls

Of forms and places that comes to life

In the middle of a sleepless night

I take embrace from quiet shadows

Revisiting lovely moments once held

Making peace with enemies held

Until to a peaceful sleep I finally doze

THE VOICE

Deep seated in the throne of emotions

Always ready to pounce

At every looming danger warn

Yet often defied and silenced

The voice that says NO

Where mistakes are already made

It stands afar tempted to probe

Did I not tell you so?

Yet no one will dare look its way

So slowly it will fades to the back

The voice that never sleeps

Willing to deliver disliked truths

Unwilling to bend nor conform

Unwilling to buy its owner's face

That lingers on behind all resistance

Never silence the voice

It leads and light your way in the dark

Truest it is more than hundred friends

Yet often it is dismissed

No matter how many times it's proven right

The voice that sits in your gut

The warning bells that rings on your path

Even unto the last leg of your fault

The God given safety siren

Never silence the voice...

TODAY I CRIED

Today I broke a promise to self

Tears dug crevices down my cheeks

Unto open streams that flowed to no end

Today I cried rivers

It was an avalanche of emotions

A surge that soaked my spirit

Breaking my will and resistance

An overwhelming moment of sadness

Today I broke down without intention

I woke up to a wet pillow, to puffy eyes

Heavy was the heart, saggy was my spirit

Tears flowed without console

Though I needed no permission to cry

I cried as if I was deprived tears for a long while

I still don't know what broke the lead

I just felt the need to cleanse my soul

UNTIL YOU FADE

Out of mind out of sight

It is a lie you still reside

Deep in my thoughts

In the core of my pulse

Though hidden the face

It is not yet ready to fade

In my mind it is planted

With deep roots anchored

Perhaps I still need to go miles

Past all the things that holds

Beyond happy moments shared

Away from the emotions felt

Until then I'll now and then pause

Each time the thought descends

Wave a little as the curtain draws

Memory by memory lock as you fade

In the deepest unmarked grave

All the thoughts I'll lay to rest

When I finally turn and wave

I'll say goodbye never to return

For now be the visitor that comes

Though without a warning nor caution

A sudden memory triggered

Be it by your sight, scent and tone

VANISHING

Love conceived in a haste

Two hearts pulled by lust

Little room left for reason

Neither to caution nor warn

Love fading like a blaze

Gallops from a heart that yearns

Dreams built on crumbling clouds

You only lasted for a while

Premature was the declaration of love

Its flakes melted just before the sun

Vanishing were the feelings claimed

They could not stand the test of times

It was a seed of love shallowly planted

Short of roots nor cause to hold

A feeling blown out of proportion

Rapidly fading without an option

WALL OF DECEIT

This wall between us

Of cold silence and sneering

Of loneliness and rejection

It was not there yesterday

This wall that divides us

It leaves my heart so sore

Too great is the divide

You so close yet too fat to reach

This tall and thick wall

It was caused by your deceit

Why did you not reach out and talked

Or whispered desires of your of heart?

We are in two sides of the world now

So divided we are by our own deeds

I, for not paying attention enough

You, for thinking I was not enough

This wall must crumble down

I wish to reach across, hold your hand

Yet my heart is too heavy to take a stand

This wall of mistrust is hard to break

WE LIVE ON

Let the blood that was spilled talk

Let the broken bones of the fallen rise

Listen oh generation that lacks an ear

Hear the voices of the departed

How fortunate you are

This freedom you've lived to see

To us it was a dream had but not held

We lived to attain but died attempting

Listen oh generation that lacks thank you

We fought so that you can be at peace

We sweat for you to know rest

We died for you to live

You say it is all in the past

Our memory is buried in yester years

Dare not fool yourselves

We live in the air of freedom you breathe

At times our spirits sorrow

Little is the value attached to the price

At times our death is made to be vain

Our names are long forgotten

Let it be known to the ears that hear

Like rain that falls to grow

Our blood still waters your tomorrow

Our voices will never be silenced by time

We will live in the air you breathe

Be a tone in the voices that dare declare

Until this freedom is complete

Our spirits will know no rest

Why should it be time that tells?

Is it not the heart that cares?

Did we not defy the odds?

Loved where there was no love

Have we not made a promise?

To hold until the end?

Why should it be up to time?

What tomorrow brings

Have you no conversed with your heart?

Mapped out what it all shall be

What if time shares not your will?

If it stops to tick tack around the clock?

Tell me here and now

Spill the contents of your heart at once

Scream your thoughts for all I care

But dare not tell me 'in time'

I am here now not down the line

Where do we stand?

Or must I go fall for time

Let him be my guy around the clock

Tick to my ear things I want to hear

Be on my wall to always behold

Or around my wrist to take along

Even on the city square for all to see